LOCKERS ARE FOR BEARCATS ONLY

LOCKERS ARE FOR BEARCATS ONLY

Mallory Tater

poems

Palimpsest Press
1171 Eastlawn Ave.
Windsor, Ontario. N8S 3J1
www.palimpsestpress.ca

Printed and bound in Canada
Cover design and book typography by Ellie Hastings
Edited by Jim Johnstone

Palimpsest Press would like to thank the Canada Council for the Arts and the Ontario Arts Council for their support of our publishing program. We also acknowledge the assistance of the Government of Ontario through the Ontario Book Publishing Tax Credit.

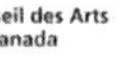

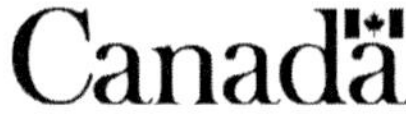

LIBRARY AND ARCHIVES CANADA CATALOGUING IN PUBLICATION

TITLE: Lockers are for Bearcats only : poems / Mallory Tater.
NAMES: Tater, Mallory, 1992- author.
IDENTIFIERS: Canadiana (print) 20260106356
Canadiana (ebook) 2026010745X

ISBN 9781997508076 (SOFTCOVER)
ISBN 9781997508083 (EPUB)
subjects: LCGFT: Poetry.

CLASSIFICATION: LCC PS8639.A855 L63 2026 | DDC C811/.6—DC23

For Curtis

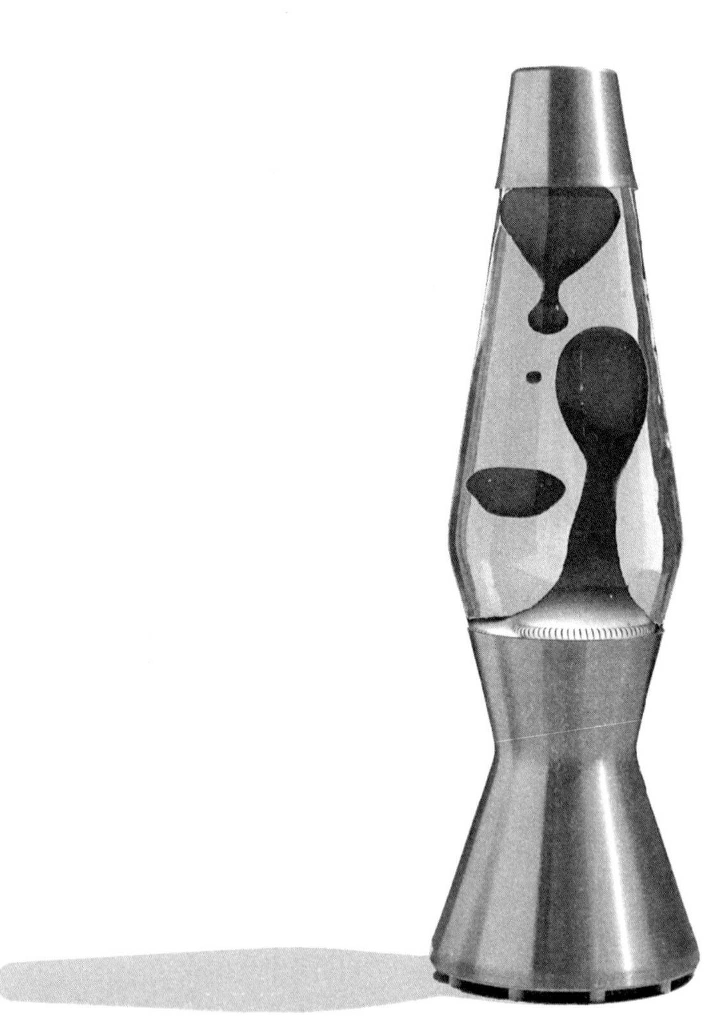

TABLE OF CONTENTS

PART ONE

PART TWO

PART THREE

PART ONE

LOCKERS ARE FOR BEARCATS ONLY

1.

Lockers are for Bearcats only
is what the underpaid fitness administrator says to me
when I ask what to do with my wallet and keys
before a length swim at the shiny new aquatic centre.

I'm charged thirteen dollars
and handed a Rubbermaid bin, its lid dripping
with water from the last crotch
out of the pool—also not a Bearcat.

2.

The renovated pool shines
like the medals wrapped
around lululemon necks
during Team Canada events I lied
about boycotting, watched on my laptop
in the dark. Because I'm a sucker
for jock lives, sweat-narratives.
I still fear them—the muscles
and intensity, how one thing
can focus a person so completely,
how much pain they are taught
to take on. How they wolf-whistle
and ice-bathe, are hazed and haze back
because it's tradition, not to be questioned.
The swish of their clothes,
the ire in their eyes. How brains tell
bodies exactly what to do
and they do it. Just do it.

3.

In the change rooms, it's Kelly, Kylie,
Kimber, Leah, Maddie,
Chelsea, Ainsley, Becca, Jordan
and Riley's world. Their damp
bathing suits and goggles clamped with silver
padlocks so as not to be stolen by wannabe Bearcats.
Their names immortalized in bubble letters
on magnetic white boards. Some are born great.
Some swim far and make forever-friends,
the same friends who doodle 90s Super S'
and spirals and shooting stars, how much they love
you while your hair dries. And through that storm
of hot wind against the brick wall, you can hear
them praise you, soak it up while your ends stop dripping.

4.

I forget my sandals, collect the Bearcats'
yesterday-hair in my toes,
run my ill-postured back under a cold shower,
drag my Rubbermaid toward the lanes.

This facility is two length pools
plus a jacuzzi I will not use because my lifeguard cousin
told me about the process of cleaning the filters,
waterlogged skin floating in the grates.

I watch parents lift their babies
into the air in the shallow end,
slide my Rubbermaid toward the bleachers,
the underworld of athletics.

I pray no Bearcats have kissed bad men behind them.

5.

My thighs are always kissing.
It took me years not to mind.

It took years off of me not to mind.
I float toward the medium lane,

water false-salted and freezing.
The Bearcats leave a windowed

meeting room, their coach
clipboarded, electrolyt,

dry-erased. Warming up,
their knees reach heaven.

Their Division One hamstrings,
number one. I scan their legs

for tattoos. The only marks,
red circles from physio cupping.

I love their matching health,
these hickies of self care,

of good will. I watch them
breathe in through their noses,

out through their mouths.
I cling to a starting block.

Out the steamed glass windows,
clusters of clouds go grey.

6.

There was a time I couldn't stop working out.
Turns out I had an "eating disorder
not otherwise specified" hibernating
in my brain and then mirrors and weights
released a willful, fractious Bearcat.
I starved. Jump-squatted. Kettle-belled. Repeated.
That gym owner, who decorated the hallways
with photos of himself hugging
Carrie Underwood and Alice Cooper,
walked around wearing gold chain necklaces
like he was the real deal. The bee's knees
of *train insane or stay the same.*
I dislocated my knee on his BOSU ball.
Is that how you spell that word?
Once, that gym's manager asked me
to take before and after photos
for their winter weight-loss campaign.
I was seventeen. I had lanugo and no one
to talk to. I desperately missed my before.
See, I could never be a Bearcat, not really.
These swimmers here and now in their jackets
flap like geese, make their way to a better
place in winter. They jump their jacks.
They're so precise. Their hands slice air.
They spider. BOSU balls are where Bearcats
statue the best! A cluster of Louise Bourgeois'
Mamans—tall, proud, unflinching, perfectly
grotesque, legs grooved with marbled muscle.
The only thing Bearcats dislocate is time
and space when they're super-duper in the zone.
They are unafraid to kill and feast, to embrace their after.

7.

I started swimming when my friend died
because it's hard to think in a line
underwater.

I wear earplugs because I am not here
to make friends or hear anyone else
make friends. I make lists. I count down.

Sometimes I list meals we haven't had in awhile.

Sometimes I list baby names.

I watch the deep-end red lines stretch
past my body and wonder what they mean.

Sometimes I name the fifty states
alphabetically or in order of restrictive
abortion laws. *Alabama, Arkansas.*

Sometimes I recite my friends' poetry.
The water, faint with salt. Shaun says,

Just because the sun is a globe of orange fire
and not an orange soda is no reason
not to enjoy your morning. I stretch

my arms over, begin to swim laps.
Selina says, *stress is just a socially acceptable*
word for fear. I'm ashamed of feeling too much.

The Bearcats burpee to their coach's
whistle, lips slicked to siren sound,
feeling everything. The whistle,
bright blue, looks like the one my sister

sent me after a free self-defense
course. Where the red line ends,
I turn around. I have to begin again.

8.

Swimming is a miracle.
The stomach is aloof.
The lungs resist.
Everything, suspended.
The heart tries.
Water slackens feet,
turns them hand-soft.
The Bearcats unzip
their jackets as they line
the elite 50-meter pool.
I watch them stare back
at themselves in the water,
smooth stray hairs
sticking out of their caps.
They circle their arms.
They crack their knuckles.
They do ledge-side
lunges without anyone
urging them to. Next,
they descend, beautiful bees
into the fast lanes.
Their team jackets,
discarded on the damp pool
ground, are plastic
grocery bags in a storm,
or each Elijah's mantles.
It's like the rapture
but they've found peace
in the deep-end. Their
bodies have not floated
to a place of nothingness.
Their bodies have earth-firm
purpose with water's

forgiveness. Their coach
tweets at them, maybe
a love song in morse code.
If I was her, how might I
whistle? What would I tell them?
Something about forevers.
Sports are full of forevers.

9.

I want you to put each other in your hearts forever!
Forever is about to happen here!
In just a few minutes!
Faster, Maddie!
Stronger, Ainsley!
Smoother, Riley!
Every lap counts, Maddie!
Make it count, Kylie!
Count it up, Chelsea!

Attack the water, Bearcats!
You are all one with the water! Leave it all behind!
Leave yourself behind!
Speed up!
Stand out!
Swim down!
Show me what you're made of!

What are you even made of?!
Come hell, be high water!
Out of the water, into your fire!
Bearcats, you are water!
We're all 70% water!
Blood is thicker than water!
Oil your troubled waters!
Or be dead in this water!

You're the driving force of your own desire!
Hurry—you're all uncharted!
Lose yourselves!
Wash yourselves away!
You do not exist but for the water!

There is a current inside each of you!
Drowns all your doubts!
Drown your past!
You are each your own tide!
You are Moses, each and every one of you
—part your own seas!
Lead that horse to the highest river!
It's time! Go! Giddy up!
Make that sorry horse drink!!

10.

A slough of sports-dads yelled at me for ten years
of my life—*Make them remember you!*
Sweat them out! Kick their butts to Pizza Hut!
Find your heat! Move your feet!
Spittle on beards, on grass, on glass.
Challenge her! during every game. I still
don't know what that means. Should I have locked
eyes with a girl on the away-team, refused to blink?
Should I have taunted her during a referee's whistle,
prophesied to her how she was going to die?
Should I have slid my gloves off, gripped her
helmet cage and growled? After the game,
should I have confronted her and her entire family
in the parking lot and keyed their van
with my Stuff by Duff keychain?
How should I have made her remember me, my heat?
How could I have kicked her butt to the closest Pizza Hut?
Instead, during games, I quoted Anne Shirley
in my head and watched the clock shrink.
I'm so glad I live in a world where there are Octobers.
In the dressing room, I changed in silence while
Gwen Stefani yelled B-A-N-A-N-A-S through a boombox
and the girls whipped sports tape at the walls.
Embarrassed at team lunches, when at Don Cherry's
Diner, teammates concocted potions with sugar cubes
and ketchup and vinegar and sprite for a server
making minimum wage to clean. My parents said
I couldn't quit—*Quitting equals sin, the dads*
are volunteers. They're trying to make you fast.
They're trying to make you good. I made one friend
on my team who loved Lord of the Rings and manga
but when everyone made fun of her for reciting
her birth date in Sindarin, I unmade the friendship.

I am not fast, certainly not good. I pray she's forgotten me. Some of the sports-dads don't speak to their daughters anymore. Statistically, that has to be true.

11.

Backstroke, ear crystals dipped in pool's
shimmer, a ringing as my reddened eyes
soak in neon lights. I can't hear
the aquasize class Dolly Parton remixes
but I know they're happening. I can only
hear saliva slicking to the back
of my throat. Shoulder sockets roll.
Arms rise. Backstroke is my first prayer
in years. There are Amens stuck
in the ceiling fans. I miss my friend
and I wish Florida and my life were different.
I like how slowly I pray this.

12.

Front crawl is where you see bodies,
band-aids on the floor, signs of life,
all that passes and all that I pass.

Flippered feet of an old man,
body of a girl beautifully
snakish, four feet below my own.

I think of us in water and in weight.
How we are what we are immersed in.
How we all might be weeping here

and no one would know.
I imagine us in an ocean
grit-green with floor-sand smoking

like fog at our collective touch.
I windmill my arms forward, keep going.
I do not watch the Bearcats.

As Dolly Parton once said,
I find out who my body is.
I do this on purpose.

13.

I'd still really like to be mistaken
for a Bearcat
                                with a locker,
                                leftover confetti
jutting at the grates from a team
birthday extravaganza.

I'd love to have a caddy full
                                of soaps
                                and healing ointments
in a place all my own.
I'd like to be a Bearcat

in a way I never could be—
                                to push,
                                use the limbs
of my body to peel back story,
dunking my torso in friendship

and butterflies and chlorine
                                where the stakes
                                are so high
that at the final meet against our rival
we'd eye of the tiger the shit out of them

and I'd be shampooed
                                with post-meet praise
                                for the wall-kick
that saved us in the final hundred
meter hell. I would be a beloved Bearcat.

14.

Bearcats don't have it all,
just one thing that everyone sees.

Bearcats live in a series of forevers
with goggle bruises under the eyes

and a language spoken in breast-strokes
and crunches. Bearcats are tired.

Sometimes they miss their moms
and their coach's eyes don't fill that gap.

But Bearcats forgive other Bearcats.
Bearcats kiss and touch their chlorine sky

whenever they need each other.
Bearcats will shake out just fine.

15.

I finish my swim, all thirty lovely minutes,
the Bearcats still warming their bodies before
they swim with a timer.

I drag the Rubbermaid
into the change room with me.

I drag the Rubbermaid
into the shower with me.

I drag the Rubbermaid
back to the benches.

I drag the Rubbermaid
into my soul

which I am pretty sure
was already made entirely of Rubbermaids.

PART TWO

ON MY FRIEND'S HOSPITAL DISCHARGE

Parousiamania is the word of the day
on my Webster's app—
Fear of the second coming of Christ—

Then I wash my face and
                                        Cora is Jesus

BEETLE

The shadow of Cora's ring
against the dark couch
looks like a beetle resting.
Sometimes she scrubs
her mind and wonders
what it would be like
to have less cleaning to do.
If instead of anxious floors
and walls, a ceiling, she could
instead have a simple floor
for a mind, littered
with grass, the idea of blood.
Not knowing what to do
with her time or knowing
what could kill us.

DUNGENESS

For Curtis

I come home to you braising pork
in stewed peppers and fat.

Cora texts me that no one special
has ever made her food,

that she's at a Mennonite diner
with her mother, ordering water

and sauerkraut. She's still sick
but I am not. You tell me

you've come to love turmeric,
that I oversalt rice when I'm drunk.

You and me, we oversalt often.
We'll be brined and well

when the banks and public parks
rot. We'll lie somewhere lovely,

iced in salt, protesting our aging
bodies, the shifting of friends.

For supper, we once slipped
into the Pacific with my grandfather's

net. We twisted our tee-shirts up
to our armpits, pretended

we could not be burned,
caught four dungeness crabs.

One pinched your wrist.
They twitched in my lunchbox.

We walked back to shore, through
algae tresses, rinsed salt off our legs

with the hose, placed the crabs
on the grass to measure which bodies

held more meat than other bodies.
I'll always want to hold you.

FOR CORA

I sweat out all my toxins in a public sauna
that reeks of car-freshener citrus.
Two women share a bench with me. Our sweat
merges in a puddle at our feet.

Yesterday you told me they took your clothes
away. Hospital security gave the doctor
four ways in which you would end your life
with the drawstrings of your sweater.
Now you're cold and the back of your body
faces an open doorway. There is a man assigned to
count your pills, watch you shower.

My fiancé lost his left toenail last week.
He walks too quickly. It jammed in a doorway.
Colour drained from his face until I think I could see you.
He retells the story in a way that omits the pain he felt,
coursing and sudden.

I see you in the women exhaling on either side of me
through a sheen of steam. *Isn't this the life?* one says.
The other wipes her thighs with a rag, clears
her throat. *Yes, I think this is it. This is the life.*

FOR CORA AGAIN

Why have I always bitten my fingernails raw?
I spend more on band-aids than books.
You text me you're in the hospital
but just for a check-up, waiting for me
to reply BULLSHIT and I do.
We've known everything
is terrible since we were forced in school
to take a Canadian Families course and learned
divorce can cause fever. The sweat stains
beneath our teacher's armpits and kneecaps.
At lunch he ate cold chicken wings alone
behind the portables. Once, he offered you
a drumstick, told you never to love
or smoke, be decent. You told me
your pug would die at age four.
He's eleven now and needs you.
I don't know that's true, but when
he scratches your mother's flower pots,
filled with daisies from your hospital stays,
he at least knows your scent.
I will place band-aids on my fingers forever.
I chew them when I'm alone without wanting to be.
You're alone without wanting to be.
You draw portraits of elderly women,
pruned and tortured and beautiful.
My favourite—her index finger bending
her lower lip open, her eyes slick
from onions or dying. I love watching you
sketch necks and chins but I'm not sure why.
One day, I ask what the woman is thinking.
You text six days later— *She's not.*
She's just like that.
She just is. I don't know.

DRUNK TEXT FROM CORA, APRIL 2012

Stay up with me
in my Jo
and my skirt
you are one
of a boy's heart
you should stay good
you have salt hair

LOCKS

Today I went to the post office
and mailed my hair to a charity.
You were in the corner
of my mind, not texting me.
Cora, if I ever get cancer,
could I wear your hair?
Or would I suddenly look
so much like you, we both
couldn't deal. I spent thirty dollars
on shampoo. It's vegan.
The hair-lady said to rub
a dime's worth into my palms
each morning, spread it evenly.
She swore to me, three times,
that if I do this my ends
will never split and my hair
will shine and my hair
will bounce subtly / long-
lastingly like a friendship
or an okay whisky
or an okay friendship
shining through stupid,
painful and brilliant summers.

CORA HATES ROLLER COASTERS

People who seek thrills
become depressed,
maybe. Cora will never
go to LA Disneyland—
her stomach has learned
to sink on its own.
When she tells us this,
we put on funeral-voices
but say it's overrated
and she will be fine.
She will be fine
without flying
to blue-and-pink land,
chewing fried foods
on sticks, hugging
a disproportionate mouse.
Cora would rather stare
at her own breasts,
lick a blade of grass,
fry us midnight eggs
and softened tomatoes
over her stove.
Cora's mouth foams
with vitamin Cs.
Cora watches bacon
as it whines and curls
slowly and without magic.

MIMOSAS

There are dresses under my sink
because Cora visited for a week
and I couldn't choose what to wear
for brunch. I hate brunch.
It's a meal where we pretend
to be happy. It's the apolitical
denial of meals.

There's a loud rumble from the parkade
that makes the couch move. It scares me.
It happens every two days. I've wanted
to ask my landlord about it
for two years. It sounds like men
howling in the pipes, shaking me.

In November 2016, the woman next door
lost her husband the same night
our world turned to louder
guns and torches and pain.
I told myself I'd leave flowers
at her door this year. To say sorry.
We're all cold and sorry.
I didn't do it. I worked seven hours
that day folding boxes. I didn't forget.
I just didn't do it.

SUMMER FLU

On the day of the eclipse,
Cora coughed up phlegm
for an afternoon.

Her body spoke.

It wasn't bright enough
or ready for the most
beautiful version of nothing.

KETCHUP HEART

There once was a girl whose pug
took a dump on the dining room table
while we were painting our nails.
There once was a girl who laughed
her entire ass off before cleaning
up after this pug. There one was a girl
who always got her hair in our cookie dough,
and, who asked, why, if a movie is 90 minutes,
that they're always over an hour?
There once was a girl who'd fold socks
with our moms and ask them about their day
while we listened to Amy Lee in our bedrooms,
ignoring our moms. There once was a girl
who played piano in the dead of night, on Bank Street,
her ballet flats stinking with dance-floor.
There once was a girl who told us she loved us so much,
her heart once turned to ketchup at the Zeller's Diner,
and it flooded toward the garden section and all around
the cheap kids toys, the cosmetics aisle. Her heart
leaked into the parking lot and reached for the Rideau River
and we all felt the tomato-warmth of it for days.
The city did not clean it up, for they felt her love too.
Her pug licked the ketchup from our arms.
We all sat perfectly still.

BEFORE OUR WEDDING

Cora wasn't feeling well when the weekend rolled
around in our mouths like frail green beans,
ends unsnipped because I am too lazy to bother.
We blanched them and ate, my phone glowing
in front of my plate. *If she doesn't make it*
to my wedding, I will not get mad, I said aloud,
but she'll give me another reason
for why it's been hard to grow up with her.
I had the flight number and refreshed
even while she and Hannah were well
up in the air, as if somehow she'd unclip
her seatbelt and float into the ether.
It's selfish, I know this. When someone you love
is too unwell to show up, how can you unmoor
your love, even for a moment?
Curtis placed a blanket over me.
I readied myself to dream.
We were already legally married, two days before.
What did it matter if Cora was there
with the roaming chickens and bottomless bacon
breakfast, Ellen leading yoga class and my god-
father chasing deer with a beer in his hand,
the forest aching with the loss of its own branches,
naked and beautiful? What did it matter?
I awoke to the sound of my phone ringing.
Hannah and Cora on the train, en route
to my apartment. When I say I ran
down the street in my pajamas without my keys
or a coat, I mean I fully ran down the street
in my pajamas without my keys or a coat.

And there she was, salt-stained boots and suitcase
with screaming wheels. We met at the crosswalk.
I wept in her arms and she laughed at me, like,
you silly girl, you know I wouldn't miss this.
I wouldn't. You know it. I love you. Grow up.

SUN GONE

With an unnaturally faint heart, I clasp
rooted qualms that match my own:
fears hidden in worn rock,
fears that rest in vertebral gaps.
Cora—she is the tallest.
She climbs in dark, and I write
our names in clay with a thin,
child-legged branch. All the way
up now; the sand and Cora's legs meld,
grit rains down from her feet
into my open mouth. I wish Cora
would fall, only in dream,
so she won't feel the rocks,
the enormity of the rocks below
where I stand and speak of things
too faint. If I could see Cora now
I'd see the winding sky has shrunk her,
but we would watch the damp
vectors of mountains.
She would pause in binding worship,
she would pause,
every reef of her bones
would pause.

I BOUGHT GRAPES

the day you died.
You'll shape me because
you have. I fell down attic stairs
and bruised my knees
after your celebration of life
but my body did not turn
as blue as your beautiful blue—
the urn that took hours to choose.
I saw you on the table.
I held your mom who said
I'll try to be her for you
and now I don't know what else to write.
The grapes shriveled on my table
but know, I ate most of them
before they expired.

ON TAKING VIA RAIL FOUR YEARS AFTER YOUR DEATH

I haven't slept on trains since you died.

Today, after four years,
I try. I'm unsuccessful but I try.

I eat Laughing Cow cheese
off my fold-down tray,

close my eyes for an hour

as a toddler plays drums with his mother,
their fold-down tray the drum kit,

their hands holding a sour rhythm.
Their songlessness weirdly rests me.

The train mists through hours of pines,

until we become stalled in Smith Falls
where we bear witness to its closed cannabis

cooperatives, the shuttered Hershey
chocolate factory, rusting trucks in ditches,

tobacco-lipped men forgetting

which of their trucks they left rusting.
We aren't far from Ottawa now, about to cross

the tracks to the place you misted
into the path of a sleeping train.

We are an hour out from that.

When we cross it, it'll be blank movement,
a nothingness in time. Songless.

Will I feel it? Hundreds of people
walk over the rusting ground where we lost you.

They cross to go to work or to leave it.

Cora, we lost you to a single
drumming train. There are many scorched

trees here, once lush, a controlled burn.
But when we go fast enough soon,

they'll still look so alive.

CORA'S PAINTING OF THE NORTHERN LIGHTS HANGS BESIDE MY TELEVISION

Most dust on furniture is dead skill cells
and grief. Pocket lint and fingernails
that throb at the sounds of trains, shed.
Heel-rind unlearning her voice,
in a vacuum universe, sucked clean.
My skin that once knew her, bathed daily,
in a time all its own. That's when I truly lose her.
When I cleanse parts of myself that once touched her.
Both of our cells, in love and once-breathing.
Somehow, we convince ourselves
we'd rather see a surface
shining ourselves back into us.
Unhealthy sparkle. Slick as shut eyes.

ANTHROPOMORPHIZING IS NORMAL, RIGHT?

I always ask if you can see me—
that you-know branch I've hung out with
near my balcony for eight months.
It shifts, tilts, nods
its chin as if it has
your chin
            —it isn't real.
But that human-ish breeze is something
I never asked for—
to make you real, post-you.
I still say hi to your branches,
their nakedness this time of year.
We saw them fuller.
                                I sure love you.
Where are you? I guess I know
in the ways that I pretend
I know anything curling above earth.
And now, I need to tilt
back into a land of reality TV,
of barbecue chips,
of singles testing their love on MTV,
though I need to know—
did you move, just then,
or are you moved
by this season finale episode?
Do you even see you?
Do you like me?
and do you even like this grief anymore?

MY GRIEF IS GETTING STRANGER

If I could clone you, I'd clone the shit out of you.
I wish I plucked your DNA
when I last saw you at my wedding,
swinging your hair to Nicki Minaj.
Now that you've died, it would be
simpler. I'd remake you. I'd go
into great debt. I'd buy your life back.
Grow you back into yourself.
I'd feed you vegetables and hold you during dark movies.
Clone-you would be so much like real-you.
Clone-you would wear dark purple make-up,
braid the seams of ripped sweaters,
drunk-dance to Carol of The Bells in June.
Clone-you would be so beautiful—
the world would turn safe for her,
like it should have tried to for you.
Clone-you would shoot pool
perfectly in ugly bars. Clone-you would
own a sweater from every American bible college
as a joke, would make elaborate bar soaps and hand them out
on the street, would paint worlds in her sleep,
never needing to stop from pain,
never dreaming of trains.

EARTHQUAKE KIT

I gorge on chickpeas, undrained and stinking,
under the bed, saved for our earthquake kit—
that day, we all anticipate
Vancouver to be ensorcelled by one stoned
and shoulder-chipped God.

Boundary Bay will draw a high fever.
Mount Baker will headache with fear.
We will hide under ourselves,
whisper we should have moved
to Pembroke or Antigonish when we got grants.

Tonight, it's not that I planned
to eat our cluster of rations—Nature Valley bars,
canned pickerel, homemade fruit leather—
it's that grief clutched me and would not let
me walk. I could not walk the serpentine

trail down Cambie Street to No Frills
for orange juice and frozen pizza.
I could not walk to Kia Foods
for kale and brown bread.
I can eat grief now. I trim wrappers with scissors,

brine my lips with small, tinned fish,
all those bones, my mouth gnathic in missing her.
I took one of her velour sweaters
from her closet. I wear it often. I did not steal
her Ariana Grande CLOUD perfume

but I sprayed it on my wrists and neck.
I did snap a photo of a photo—her beautiful childhood
self on a toboggan—
gap-toothed, forever-girl, winter
splashed on her cheeks. When we were girls

we'd weave our hair together until we were conjoined,
we'd wear g-strings and tell lies to our moms,
we'd tell lies about ourselves to each other
under the glow of lava and ice fiber lamps,
all because we were bored and breathing.
My survival has become silent—

it's not legumes, an emergency radio, AA batteries.
I am not afraid of The Big One.
I am not afraid of some drunk God.
I am afraid of what I can do without her.
And how she can't see me doing it.

NATURE'S BOUNTY VITAMINS

On the day of your celebration
of life, Hannah gave me
vitamins to improve my nails
and hair. Gummies she said
cost thirty dollars
and she had been so silky
and happy with how her hair
fell and how her nails firmed.
They tasted surprisingly good.
I sucked on the soft pink candies
swollen with health—
D, and C, and omega 3s—
while we didn't do our eye makeup.
We decided against touching our eyes.
All four of us, your best girls,
holding blush brushes
to our faces, mascara-less,
tired of crying for you.
We'd cry this moment until it
blackened and no one wanted
to remove it. We all fell
and firmed. Cora, we'll all fall
and firm to try nothing,
to try health, to try to not keep
thinking of you
while still always thinking of you.

GO UN-BE NOW

I loved you.
You loved me.

You're not here.
I am still trying

to make that real
in my brain.

My brain can hold
the world, I think,

until it can't,
until you're gone.

You're in that tree
by my house

and you can't
convince me otherwise.

You move, move,
and move,

twitch, rustle
on Wednesdays

as if you hadn't
already lived

through enough pain,
enough of people

asking you to try.
I ask you to speak

in wind
and I know it's wrong.

We never had
a handshake.

But we spelt
our love out—

we could spell it
in the air

when you'd kiss
my cheek

or say you don't
want to be here

and I'd try to sow
the seed of that—

you wanting to un-be.
Nothing grew.

I think that's okay.
So when I ask you

to show me in the trees
that you're listening,

It's okay. Ignore me.
Don't move.

Don't move at all.
I love you.

I may be selfish.
Please rest.

PART THREE

ANIMALS

A swarm of bees
A stream of minnows
An ascension of larks
A cast of hawks
A forgiveness of girls

ACORN CLUB

My favourite tree growing up was a birch
against whose trunk our yellow labrador
Mabel lost a toenail. She was chasing
a squirrel. The tree was simply breathing.
On the same birch, I peeled off skin
and chalked small notes, get well's for Mabel
and sent messages to my sisters—
slid them under their bedroom doors.

My least favourite tree growing up
was near my house too. The tree,
thick, tensed with acorns, housed
older children, with whom I was not welcome.

The acorn tree had goth fingernails
and many hands. It would not
hold mine. It had a floorboard
laid at its peak
where the teens would tan and smoke.
It held conversations about Mentos in Pepsi,
hand-jobs in sheds, mean boys
with their slurs and their hurt.
The tree's bark smelled like fireworks,
freshly lit, about to shoot off
into the sky's big mouth,
punch its lights out.

Alone, unwelcome, on earth's peeling paper,
I'd write to my sisters who also did not belong—
Wanna find Mabel's nail?
It was her left paw. It's stopped bleeding.
Wanna pretend we don't hear them up there?
Circle Y, Circle N.

PURITY RING

The two boys sifted for Thomas' purity ring in the grass for an hour. Thomas had let Ethan wear it because yesterday was dress rehearsal for the school play and Ethan played a married man. The ring had a gravel-textured dove carving at the centre and was blessed by a migrant youth pastor from Albuquerque. Thomas had trusted Ethan. They were cousins. Ethan lost the ring sometime during the six mile run in P.E. class. *"Your fingers are fatter and I was sweaty."*

Thomas thought his father would kill him—it had cost an extra seventy dollars to have the thing blessed. The grass around the track was stringy and warm and moist. Thomas squatted and felt the dew wet his legs.

A team of boys ran by the two cousins. They passed a blue baton as they sprinted in a line. Their pinnies flapped violently. Ethan soon saw something shining in the dirt beside a pylon.

Thomas had given up before Ethan told him this. He stared at the sun.

WE DAUGHTERS SUCK BLUEBERRIES ON THE EDGE OF ALOUETTE ROAD, 1996

The parish mother's group stands outside a prison. I am four years-old, stop signs painted on my cheeks by other parishioners. They protest another woman's sentence. She'd chained her body to the doors of an abortion clinic and got detained over the holidays. Mrs. N with a fetus on her shirt, outstretches her hand, *you're a miracle, what if a woman, your mother, had killed you?*

We daughters suck blueberries on the edge of Alouette Road. I don't want to be here and I know this at four. Or my memory tells me this later.

I'll stay in this memory for women I love. It won't have a firm girlhood. It will braid and bind around the heads of women who are afraid and chant *the lord is here, the Lord is here.*

At noon it rains. My facepaint bleeds onto my hand. Wind hushes paper signs into gutters, forces the parish back into their vans. These mothers are silenced, tired. I feel bad but I am thankful.

A week later, that woman will be released from her cell. A priest will force me to make her a Thank You card at our dining room table. The woman will walk home until her feet hurt.

BIBLE SCHOOL HEAT DREAM

"Keep the barns dry and the birds warm."
— *Global News* Headline during BC floods, 2021.

Keep that end of August air
bloated with smoke, brine and morning,
one I know infinitely well from decades
of being in the pacific northwest.

So why does my scent memory reject
plunging me toward the family cabin,
grandpa's hand-shark fin behind sand bars,
grilled corn, garlic salads tossed by hand,

my sister's salt-licked hair under my chin?
Instead, August air pushes my memory
ditch-side, puking cheerios and apologies
toward Canadian megachurches

and a pastor's matching daughters
megaphoned and chicken-dancing.
I'm brought back to being weighed down
by a Christ I don't believe in, prayer

chains and tears for places outside of us.
We bibled parts of ourselves away
and the *na-na-na-na-na-na-na-na-na*
of it all makes me feel filthy.

August air brings me back to vacation bible school.
I see the latex gloves of women passing out
one o'clock oreos, how I twist the top wafer off,
easy in the heat, lick the white host of frosting

and pray for absolutely nothing, except
for everyone here to stop being so afraid
and yet so loudly, loudly sure.
It's August again. The barns will not stay dry.

The birds will all be flu-borne. Those pastor's
daughter's names still crested in my mouth.
I might spit them into the heat.
I will never learn how forgiveness works.

ST. BLAISE DAY

My school was so Catholic we celebrated
St. Blaise Day each February—
Saint of Afflictions of the Throat.
I shit you not.
                    The priest would place criss-
crossed candles, unlit, under our chins
and bow. In the name of the Father,
and of the Son, and Stephanie still got sick
and spread it to Katie, Angela, Dylan, me.
We coughed and wiped snot on our blouses.
We coughed loudly until God heard us.

I used to think of St. Blaise during oral sex,
something so strong in my mouth,
my crimped hair shying in front of my eyes.
Who is the saint of giving good head?
Who is the saint of consent?
And where is the saint that tells young girls
we can say no within the confessional
of washroom stalls?

I WALK BY MY OLD PARISH

The church is embalmed with a wind-swept crust—
peeled paint, puffs of dead wheat, gravel ground
by the teeth of the odd tractor. You can taste the roof,
the steeple of the church once shellacked and polished
regularly by settlers seeking god, its shingles now
loosened and dampened by warm summer rain.
It's abhorrent, the taste in the air, like if lightning
was poured in a glass of bleach and warm rust.
I haven't seen this place in years. I imagine
its soon-future where tornados will be impossibly
often and everywhere. The breath of them will smash in
the doves, kill them all in one foul swoop. I do not
mean real doves. I mean the the glass flocks
in the centre of each stained-glass window.
When I was young, me and my sisters trying not to sleep
through the Monsignor's homilies, we'd name the birds
in our heads. On the drive home, stale donuts in our laps,
we'd share our lists, vote on whose name won that Sunday—
Daffy Duck, Ballsack, Darth Vader, Puddles.
And we can now confirm that there will be a world where
these named doves are dead, their bodies shattered,
a world where there is no second chance and no second coming.
There will be nothing to win, as real birds take flight,
their gray and white bodies in air, nothing to tell
them apart from debris in our sorry mind's eyes.

FIRST COMMUNION

You have a big tongue
is what the priest who gives me
my first communion says to me
as he shakes my grandfather's hand
by the white statue of Mary,
her head bent in shame or prayer.

I feel my words on the roof
of my mouth, my breath still glutinous
with my first taste of Christ
and hungry because it did not feel
like anything. My white surplus
blows in the wind and I stand

in front of the virgin, bow
my head like she does. The priest
and my grandfather watch
as my mother snaps a photo of me,
alone, the wooden cross snaked
around my neck, tucked into my shirt.

We do a retake with the cross
on the outside of my gown
at my mother's request.
Christ is on top of your heart now,
you'll want to remember it like that.
When I look at this photograph

wrinkled from living in a box
of memories my parents gave to me
when they downsized, I do not see Christ—
I see a girl with so much love to give,
a bad haircut, a headband with cold
hard teeth digging into my crown.

I see my hands clasped in prayer,
closed off, pointing toward the men
who are not in the frame,
who are no longer alive,
and whose words should have never
meant everything.

SPIRIT

My understanding of alcoholism
is that your body becomes the bottle.

We fill and drain.
I am an idle, imminent well.

My ancestor's hands shake. I pour a glass
of seltzer. My grandfather, too, tried

to heal with clean, carbonated beverages.
I am too old. One time, my mom recalls

the day she earned a wrinkle between her brows—
she was changing the baby.

I was fighting with a friend who tricked me
into the yard, locked me out in minus forty.

Mum says she saw me in the snow,
barefoot, bath-damp hair turning to ice

at the tips. She says I wrapped my arms
and legs around silver maple,

committed unyieldingly to cold,
pressed my stomach to sap. *And I called for you.*

You didn't move. I called three times.
I know you heard me. You must've heard me.

HANGOVER

I have time I don't want. Sometimes I don't want
to carry myself to the point of no fresh vegetables,
no bread. But it's so beautiful, the sight of my breath,
trying. I want to sip every puddle on Main Street,
lick my lips with the snow flurries we post about
with dread, peer through every church window,
remember they were places I once needed.
Crosses mark skies and graves impressively.
I want to mark myself with expensive tattoos,
feathers turning to birds in search of missing feathers—
sometimes you have to be pulled backwards to be
propelled forward even further. This winter I learned
the correlation between libido and saving heat—
This too shall pass.

THIGH GAP, EARLY ANOREXIA RECOVERY

It's 2012 when I finally learn to eat a sandwich
without removing the bread,
building it
into an angry ball

in my palms
and pitching it into the garbage.

It turns out I love mayonnaise
and for the first time in a while, I hang out

with friends and walk the dog and go
to lots of movies.

At the Rideau Centre mall
we're shopping

and the salesperson at Aritzia says to my friend—

Your legs are candy canes.
They're perfect.

I look down at the flesh
I was told would bring back my period.

We all look at the girl.

My friend tells us
about a machine at Good Life,

how it's changed her life.

I stop talking to my friend for an hour.
We don't buy matching TNA sweaters.

I was wrong and I am sorry.

BULIMIA IS STILL HARD TO WRITE ABOUT

I remember at seventeen,
my orange fingers
shove barfed Cheetos
down my parents'
bathroom sink. Our pipes
do not work well enough
to hide how sick I am.
I sprinkle Drano until
the basin is white
and empty again.
The toxic pebbles smell
like formaldehyde.
I embalm the act of losing,
turn the fan on, dim
the lights, close the pine door,
the sunset stained on my mouth.

FLATTERING

The beautiful woman
at the bridal store,
with a bowl cut
and distressed
clogs, walks me
to a mirror world.

Wow—your hips
are invisible in this.
It's just so flattering.
It's like where
did you even go?
Where are you?
Where are you?

FASTING GIRLS

On farms with sheep,
their fleece moldy with winter, and bruised
barn cats with the blood of
mice in their guts, lived tons of Victorian girls
who did not eat. They said the Lord had taken over
their bodies, that he would feed them
his word and his heart. The girls' mothers and farmhands,
at first, would spoon their daughters and sisters porridge
at night, trick them into eating in dream.
The girls would spew and scream awake,
their bellies filled to the brim
with the roars of God, they'd claim.
Blue-lipped mothers would come to believe
their Nelly's and Anna's and Daisy's
so firmly, a divine light would enter
the home as the girls' wrists and ankles, barbed
with vein, unfleshed and rotted.
The girls' throats would become
scorched by prayer and no broth
as their mothers sat by fires
sipping smoke, rosary beads
leaving marks in their palms.
Priests from villages miles away
would visit the girls before they died,
bless them in their white nightgowns
that clouded what was left.
I learn of Fasting Girls on Wikipedia
when I am in my thirties
and no longer spending days, mouth watering
for chicken wings and toast, mana
from my own sense of heaven. I am well
when I learn of these girls who ingested psalms

about the wicked, baked and oiled
into the stoves of their mother's eyes.
Were we once Fasting Girls,
falsely saint-like for locking
ourselves in our rooms during meals?
Canonized for thigh gaps,
sanctified with anemia.
I once did not eat for two days,
and fell into a snowbank
on a walk home from a sleepover
with other Fasting Girls. Truly
I tell you, that night
I was so hungry,
I sat there, and almost
licked dirt from the ice.

ELVIS STOJKO DOES A DOUBLE LUTZ

in a gold mesh top at the 38th annual Stars on Ice Tour.
He is fifty-two and the crowd wilds for him.
If I twisted and bent my body for a living,
I would be so tired and rude all of the time, aching.
I wish I could fly like Elvis Stojko.

Tonight I put on a thin top
from a thrift store in Hintonburg.
The light through the branches, mesh.
Winds whipped a tree on our street in half.
A branch dangles from its own shoulder socket.
My spouse called the city about it. They didn't answer.
We are not the only ones who sustain injury, whose bodies fail.
They should care, Curtis said. It's their tree.

We walk for food under this hazard.
Someone in their apartment next to it
sees nothing, warms their hands over their dinner.
Cold air breathes through my top.
I never dress well for what's next.

The Dog Meister stand is still open.
They have homemade relish.
We twist and lean over the gutter in unison,
napkins wrapped around soggy kaiser buns.
Behind us, the moon, a frailty.
The moon and us and the tree and Elvis Stojko
aging, aching, glorious.
We eat until we are full.

I THINK MY BIRTHDAY WAS YESTERDAY

Our apartment parkade reeks of rotting pears, of eggplant skin, salmon bones, wet weed. A new sign on our blue bins—*Do Not Misuse Me—NO BOOKS—hardcover, paperback, magazines in with the cardboard. It lessens the worth of the cardboard.* Cardboard being worth something to someone is a thought that cramps my wrists—that muscle twitch, bone lethargy, when something is soft enough to be sad. *NO hard plastic with soft plastic. Follow the building online for updates.* Our building has X. I toss away our empty olive oil, vinegar jar, yesterday's beer bottles, the bootlegging of peace to our brains. I toss all the empties to join more empties in fullness.

I remember being a child collecting trash in a time I thought was special and mine—starfish skin glossed with clear nail polish to preserve it, a turtle carapace I found trespassing onto a military golf course, paid ten dollars to have polished by a skate sharpener guy in a mall. I used to grab long white feathers in parking lots, wilted and dirtied with airborne shit—a child sees the world as a series of gifts. A child only knows in birthdays.

I follow our building. I hold my phone while I sleep.

PODCAST LULLABIES

Since the world buckled and we all
hushed with fear, lived behind
our quiet walls for four plus years,
I cannot sleep without voices in my ears.
I depart the world each night at eight-thirty,
listen to American strangers tell me about
teenage mothers in Indiana,
the middle child from Full House's memoir
that may not have been ghost-written,
how Laura Ingalls Wilder was actually
convinced by her daughter, Rose,
to write her childhood into books
so Rose could afford to drink in High Society England.

With my rose headphones planeting my ears,
I sink into an ocean of tabloid gossip,
a sky of unsolved murders.
I fall asleep mid-story, mid-sentence,
until my dreams are problematic faves
and I don't know you're next to me by morning.
You're always here, a voice I can so well pin
to a kind face. Sometimes you snore. I don't mind.

I foster these deep friendships, one-sided,
with people who couldn't pick me out of a crowd
but whom I fall asleep with every night.
If I ever met Liz or Claire, Princess or Glynnis,
I'd tell them I love them and that when my room
is night enough, I see them as my dresses
blowing with the fan's breath, that their voices
wash forward a calmness in me, how they don't know
it but, like you, they take me gratefully, sonically back
toward uncertain street lamps.

ON RECEIVING BAD NEWS

We, women, grew hungry, ate from a pile
of unassuming, pleasant rocks. They fell
into our mouths, slipped into the blankness
of our bodies. Some of them cut our throats.
We truthed most things in life that were sharp
and so we said it was our fault. The rocks
I sucked and swallowed, little still insects
I sent to my body, to heal myself
from the stomach outward, back into the world
if I could digest. We dared each other
to digest. I hoped the rocks could venture
to my toes, give me the dull ache of a stance.
Maybe the earth has an answer
and we don't ingest it. I hoped I'd choke up
these pebbles one day when I need to hear
my own voice, when I need to remember
the weight of being a woman, of being.
We ingested all we could beside a lake
with no name, no cabins dripping off the shore
with their loud wealth and wood. It was five
o'clock and dark. No one was watching.
No one was watching us fill ourselves and live.
Once we filled ourselves, we swore we'd live.

ON RECEIVING GOOD NEWS

For Monica

Once we hang up our phones,
I eat oatmeal, watch the world
on CNN sink and recess, sink, reset.
At the bus stop, I stand beside
two women. Each pushes a stroller,
their babies blanketed from rain.
Twice, the women lift their blankets,
adjust the hats on their baby's ears.
They do not see each other.
After this, I swim a mile
in my bright, cracked community pool,
bodies seemingly rashed and lonely.
I stretch my hips, starfishing
in the deep-end. Sixty-five-year-old women
in bathing caps and baggy t-shirts
say hello, that I am welcome—
I have crashed senior hour.
When you called me and said
you were going to be a mother,
I was so sure and awake as anything—
everything that knew brightness saw me.
I became daffy, adrift with hope.
I could not see straight and I did not want to.
So I swim a mile with these women.
We do not rush. I think you gave us the sun.

A VERY TWILIGHT POEM

I make you feed me
lines from Twilight when I am sad.

Bella, we're making Italiano for you.
You fry garlic, oily ground beef.

On the news, the meteorologist
from Global TV tells us that the rain

will not cease. I will not cease
to utter *say it, say it out loud,*

when the bar is closing
and you tell me how much our bill is.

You're always reading these days.
Facts carried home and pinned

to our walls like immortally
collected graduation caps, ironic and blue.

Tonight, you plate our dishes with red sauce,
crack the pepper thoroughly.

Say it, say it out loud.

SISTERHOOD OF THE TRAVELING

1.

Four girls who aren't real
glitter a pair of jeans.
The cuffs conflicted
with sequins, the knees
faded from longing.
Four girls weep
on the loopholes,
dream down the fly,
bleed on back rivets.

The pants belt the girls
together during
a summer apart.
They wear them
on soccer fields,
at Shakespeare camp,
department store
break-rooms.

On the knees
the girls pen
names of men
they love
in bed
and in passing.

2.

One summer I am friendless,
too thin, tired. I join these four girls.

    I'm with Bridget in Turkey,
    pouring whisky into her mouth,
    braiding her forever-hair.
    She finds bones
    of an ancient mother,
    and I listen to her story
    about her mother's
    miscount of pills.

Lena returns to Santorini
for the love of a man
who isn't there.
But I'm there,
kissing her zitless face.
We soak phyllo dough
in her grandmother's basin
filled with olive oil.
I tell her I love her.

    Carmen needs to breathe.
    Her parents have learned family
    without her. We throw a rock
    in her father's kitchen window
    in Charleston, South Carolina
    and maybe we throw rocks
    in all suburban kitchens,
    hear them disturb white dishes
    in off-white farmhouse sinks.

Tibby might have it the toughest.
Tibby befriends a very sick girl
when she faints at the market.
Tibby also has a pregnancy scare.
She lets me join her on a shift.
We stick prices on shampoos
and wallets until we can't breathe
but we do and smoke a joint,
exhale, speak of loss later.

3.

The four girls pay for my flight to Greece
for the final week of August.
So we can be together, they say!
Jet-lagged, we magically become five.
At night we walk to the marina in Oia where
the moon is a she and she is everything.

There, the girls hand me the pants,
Wear them
they'll make you brave.
I stick my sand-crusted feet
through the pant legs.
They're too long.
They're too tight.
They don't fit.
The fly won't do up, my hips are sucked
and in pain, and the jeans
drag and drag along the wet teak dock.

The girls, speechless, squint at Cycladic houses,
built longer ago than our brains can hold.
They ask me *what did you do wrong?* with their shoulders
before they say *it's okay, it's okay.*
I remove the pants.
The magic loosens,
a necessary oil spill
dripping through dock cracks.
The girls decide they're actually more mad
at the pants than they are at me.
And I love this for them.
I love them for me.

In our underwear,
we climb down the marina
ladder from land
toward the infinite blue
of whatsername sea.
Bridget doesn't take the stairs,
jumps instead, blonde hair spreading
out like a jellyfish breathing.
We tread water, hold hands
and hum Chantal Kreviazuk.

The water, freezing, slows
our song. Our chests
all hollow with cold. We collectively lose
our thoughts. We shiver. We turn blue.
A local fisherman helps us onto his boat.
He carries us
one by one back to the dock.
The pants lay there covered in sand.
We twitch like choked fish beside them.
Lena's yia-yia runs down the dock.
She weeps over our bodies.
We all have hypothermia.
I can't feel it but I know the four of us
are holding hands.

As emergency paramedics hover
over each of us, and gulls flap
above us like we are prey,
Greek men on the horizon
hauling in their catch
as if we don't exist,
in our silver, emergency blankets,
we match, so perfectly bright.
The same.

NOTES

"A Very Twilight Poem" was published in *Maisonneuve*, Spring 2025.

"Cora's Painting of the Northern Lights Hangs Beside My Television" was published in *The Malahat Review*, 2024.

"Spirit" and "Thigh Gap, Early Anorexia Recovery" were published in *Contemporary Verse 2*'s Addiction Issue, Spring 2023.

"Sisterhood of the Traveling" and "Animals" were published in *poetrycanada* in 2022.

"Anthropomorphizing is Normal, Right?," "Locks," "My Grief is Getting Stranger," "Nature's Bounty Vitamins" and "St. Blaise Day" were published in *Room Magazine*'s Hair Issue in 2020.

"Flattering" was published in Biblioasis' *Best Canadian Poetry* in 2019.

"Beetle," "Cora Hates Roller Coasters," "Dungeness," "For Cora," "For Cora Again," Mimosas," and "Summer Flu" were published in *The Capilano Review* in 2019,

"On Receiving Bad News" was published online in *Room Magazine*'s Issue of canlitaccountable in 2016.

"Sun Gone" was published by *Contemporary Verse 2* in 2015.

In "Lockers Are for Bearcats Only," the lines *"stress is just a socially acceptable word for fear. I'm ashamed of feeling too much."* are taken from Selina Boan's "From All You Can Is the Best You Can," originally published in *Undoing Hours* (Nightwood Editions, 2021) and Poetry in Voice.

In "Lockers Are for Bearcats Only," the lines *"Just because the sun is a globe of orange fire and not an orange soda is no reason not to enjoy your morning."* are taken from Shaun Robinson's originally published "Sunomono" in *If You Discover a Fire* (Brick Books, 2021) and The Rusty Toque.

THANK YOUS

Thank you to Jim Johnstone for your editorial encouragement and generous time on this manuscript. I am so fortunate to work with you. Thank you to the Palimpsest, Anstruther and River Street folks for taking good care of my work during the publication process, especially Aimee, Ellie and Hollay. Thank you to the BC Arts Council. Thank you to The UBC School of Creative Writing for your support and community, especially to Sheryda, Tanya, Mandy and Zac.

Carter, Chris, Clara, Jasmine, Jess, Jocelyn, Kyle, Megan, Mica, Molly, Rachel, Selina, Shaun, and wâpanatâhk — it's an honour to share in your writing and friendships.

Thank you to Selina, Domenica and Ambrose for spending time with my work and sharing your thoughtful words and support for this book.

Gratitude and love to my Tater and LeBlanc families. And always, to Margot, Rachelle, Joanna and our Lauren. Jennifer, Simon and family: My sincere thankfulness and respect—your continued presence in our lives means the world.

Lastly: Curtis, Curtis, Curtis. Flossie, Flossie, Flossie. You're both everything. You're all of it. And I love you both so much.

Mallory Tater is the author of *This Will Be Good: Poems* (Book*Hug Press, 2018), *The Birth Yard: A Novel* (HarperCollins, 2020), and *Soft Tissue: A Novel* (forthcoming, ECW Press, 2027). She was the publisher of Rahila's Ghost Press, a now-retired chapbook press. Mallory currently lives in Vancouver, where she teaches at the University of British Columbia's School of Creative Writing. This is her second poetry collection.